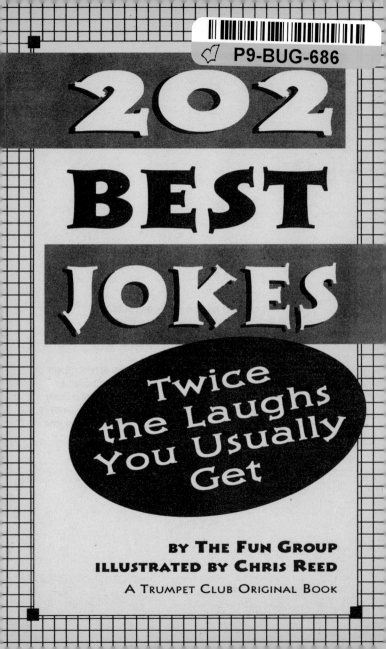

P9-BUG-686

202 BEST JOKES

Twice the Laughs You Usually Get

BY THE FUN GROUP
ILLUSTRATED BY CHRIS REED

A TRUMPET CLUB ORIGINAL BOOK

Published by The Trumpet Club
1540 Broadway, New York, New York 10036

Copyright © 1993 Parachute Press, Inc.

All rights reserved. No part of this book may be reproduced or
transmitted in any form or by any means, electronic or
mechanical, including photocopying, recording or by any
information storage and retrieval system, without the written
permission of the Publisher, except where permitted by law.

ISBN: 0-440-83044-3

Printed in the United States of America
May 1993

1 3 5 7 9 10 8 6 4 2
OPM

CONTENTS

Ten Steps to Take Before You Read This Book   5

These Jokes Are So Old, They're History!   7

These Jokes Are Monsters   12

These Jokes Will Make You Cross   19

Jokes, Jokes, and—Guess What—More Jokes!   21

Let's Boot These Crazy Computer Jokes!   27

Bananas, Burgers, and Other Foods   29

Knock-Out Knock Knocks   36

Be a Sport!   39

Jason Priestly's Home Phone Number*   81

These Jokes Are Sick   44

Animal Howls   48

Do-It-Yourself Jokes   57

Two Too Cruel   60

More Knock-Out Knock Knocks   62

School Jokes with Class   66

Riddle-diculous Riddles   73

* Psych! Made you look!

TEN STEPS TO TAKE BEFORE YOU READ THIS BOOK

You are about to read 202 of the funniest jokes of all time! To get into the proper mood for hysterical laughter, we recommend this **Ten-Step Wacky Workout Program....**

1. Go to an antique store and ask, "What's new?"

2. Visit a laundromat and ask, "What's the latest dirt?"

3. Go to an aquarium and say, "Something's fishy here."

4. Visit a skin doctor. Tell the doctor not to do anything rash.

5. Visit a bike store. Ask to see the spokesperson.

6. Visit a dentist and ask, "What are you trying to pull?"

7. Visit a magician and ask, "How's tricks?"

8. Go ice fishing. Be sure to throw back any cubes you catch that are too small.

9. Get in shape; a trapezoid is a good one.

10. Say "Ah" backward three times.

See, you're laughing already! Now you're ready for the **202 Best Jokes of All Time.**

THESE JOKES ARE SO OLD, THEY'RE HISTORY!

Q: Which Civil War general wore the largest hat?

A: The one with the largest head!

Q: What did Ben Franklin say when he discovered electricity?

A: "I'm shocked!"

Pam: You probably won't believe it, but I spent eight hours over my history book last night.

Sam: You were studying for eight hours?

Pam: No. I put it under my bed!

Teacher: What important event happened in 1809?

Matt: Abraham Lincoln was born.

Teacher: That is correct. And what important event happened in 1812?

Matt: Abraham Lincoln had his third birthday!

Q: Why are the Middle Ages called the Dark Ages?

A: Because there were so many knights.

First Kid: I was named after Abraham Lincoln.

Second Kid: Your name is Abraham?

First Kid: No. It's Josh.

Second Kid: Then how could you be named after Abraham Lincoln?

First Kid: He was named in 1809, and I was named in 1982!

Pam: Why was George Washington buried at Mount Vernon?

Sam: Because he was dead.

Q: Where were the kings and queens of England crowned?

A: On their heads.

Pa: How did Sam do on his history test?

Ma: Not too well. But it wasn't Sam's fault. They asked him about things that happened before he was even born!

Matt: On December 6, 1742, 45 people walked out of the best restaurant in Paris, France. Do you know why?

Sam: No. Why?

Matt: They'd finished eating!

Q: How long was Andrew Jackson in the White House?

A: About five feet ten inches long.

Pam: Why did George Washington always sleep standing up?

Sam: Because he couldn't lie!

**ONLY 67
MORE PAGES
TILL YOU GET TO
THE WORLD'S
DIRTIEST JOKE!**

THESE JOKES ARE MONSTERS

What kind of music does a mummy like best?
Wrap music.

How did the monster get a part in the movie?
He took a scream test.

Little Girl Monster: Mommy, the teacher says I'm nice, smart, and well-behaved.
Mommy Monster: Well, I hope you do better next term!

What is a monster's favorite TV show?
Beverly Chills 90210.

Who is a monster's favorite star?
Jason Beastly.

Why are skeletons such cowards?
They have no guts.

Monster Kid: I hate my teacher's guts.

Mommy Monster: Well then, leave them on the side of the plate and just eat your vegetables.

What are ghost kids' favorite toys?
Boo-merangs.

Why couldn't the monster go to college?
His extension cord wasn't long enough.

Why do ghosts go to the amusement park?
To ride the roller ghoster.

Where do most ghosts live?
At dead ends.

What's the scariest tall building in the world?
The Vampire State Building.

Why does Frankenstein like old jokes?
They keep him in stitches.

Why did Frankenstein go to see a psychiatrist?
He had a screw loose.

Why did it take Frankenstein three hours to finish a 200-page book?
He wasn't very hungry.

Monster Boyfriend: I'm here to ask for your daughter's hand in marriage.
Daddy Monster: No way. You take all of her, or it's no deal.

Why did the ghost become a cheerleader?
To show off her school spirit.

Monster: I don't feel well. I have a cold.

Monster Doctor: Just take some coffin drops.

What does a monster say to a three-eyed, scaly green zombie with no teeth and ratty purple hair?
"Hey good-looking!"

Where do ghosts like to spend their vacations?
At Club Dead.

How does a monster count to 17?
On his fingers.

First Zombie: Let's have a party.
Second Zombie: Okay, who should we invite?
First Zombie: Anyone we can dig up.

Why didn't Dracula's cousin climb back in his coffin at sunrise?
He was an all-day sucker.

What would you get if you crossed a vampire bat with a magician?
A flying sorcerer.

What do you call a monster who's ten feet tall?
Shorty.

Do vampires have holidays?
Sure. Haven't you ever heard of Fangsgiving?

Mother Monster: Do you think we should take Junior to the zoo?
Father Monster: No dear. If the zoo wants him they'll just have to come and get him.

THESE JOKES WILL MAKE YOU CROSS

Q: What do you get when you cross a computer with a crab?

A: Snappy answers!

Q: **What do you get when you cross an elephant with a mouse?**

A: A very large hole in your wall!

Q: **What do you get when you cross a banana with a hyena?**

A: Peels of laughter!

Q: **What do you get when you cross a rock with a dog?**

A: A rock that chases itself around the yard!

Q: **What do you get when you cross a giraffe with a rooster?**

A: An animal that wakes up the people on the top floor!

JOKES, JOKES, AND—GUESS WHAT?—MORE JOKES!

Will: Why haven't you changed the water in the goldfish bowl?

Bill: They haven't finished what's in there yet!

Bill: My dog doesn't have a tail.

Will: **Then how do you know when he's happy?**

Bill: He stops biting me!

Will: Well, my dog doesn't have a nose.

Bill: **Then how does he smell?**

Will: Terrible!

Sam: **Do you have difficulty making up your mind?**

Pam: Well . . . yes and no.

Q: **What becomes shorter when you add two letters?**

A: The word "short."

Q: **What goes up but never comes down?**

A: Your age!

Q: What can you break with a single word?

A: Silence.

Officer (*to driver in parked car*):
Didn't you see that sign—"Fine for Parking"?

Driver: Yes, I saw it, and I fully agree with it!

A man hurried angrily into the electrician's shop. "I called you yesterday morning to send someone to fix my doorbell," he roared. "You promised to send a man over at once. What happened?"

"But we sent someone!" the manager insisted. He turned to Joe, his assistant. "Didn't you go round to the Smiths' yesterday?"

"Sure I did," said Joe. "I went over there, and I rang the doorbell for fifteen minutes, but I didn't get an answer!"

Will: I lost my dog last week.
Bill: **Why don't you put an ad in the paper?**
Will: It wouldn't do any good. He can't read.

Wife: Where's yesterday's paper?

Husband: I wrapped the garbage in it.

Wife: But I didn't even get to see it!

Husband: You didn't miss anything. Just a lot of coffee grounds and some apple cores.

Pam: If you don't stop playing that harmonica, I'll go crazy!

Sam: Too late. I stopped an hour ago!

April: Where's your new guitar?

May: I had to throw it away.

April: You threw it away? Why?

May: It had a hole in the middle!

April: Was that you singing when I came in?

June: Yes. I was killing time before my next singing lesson.

April: Well, you're using the right weapon!

June: Don't you think my singing
voice has improved?

April: It's improved, but it's not cured.

Pam: Is that your brother?

Sam: Yeah.

Pam: He's very short, isn't he?

Sam: Well, he's only my half-brother.

LET'S BOOT THESE CRAZY COMPUTER JOKES!

Q: How do you eat a computer?
A: One byte at a time.

Mother: Matt, I'm worried that you're overdoing it with that computer of yours. You've been sitting in front of the screen for four hours straight!

Matt: It's okay, Mom. It isn't plugged in.

Q: How do computers know what they want to eat?

A: They read the menu.

Q: What button should you press when your computer starts to shake and whistle?

A: The panic button.

Will: I wish I had the money to buy the world's most expensive computer.

Bill: Why do you want the world's most expensive computer?

Will: I don't. I just want the money.

BANANAS, BURGERS, AND OTHER FOODS

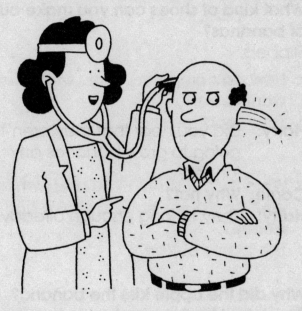

Doctor: My heavens you must be upset! You have a banana growing out of your ear!

Patient: You bet I'm upset. I *planted* squash.

What's yellow and mushy and you can write with it?
A ballpoint banana.

What kind of shoes can you make out of bananas?
Slippers.

Harry: Did you hear that they aren't going to grow bananas any longer?
Carrie: Why not?
Harry: They're long enough already.

Why did the apple kiss the banana?
Because it had appeal.

How do you turn a banana into a vegetable?
Stomp on it and make it squash.

If an apple a day keeps the doctor away, what does an onion a day do?
Keeps everyone away.

What's green and has its own postage stamp?
Elvis Parsley

How do you make a strawberry shake?
Force it to watch a horror movie.

How can you make a hot dog cold?
Cover it with chili.

How do you make meat loaf?
Send it on vacation.

Diner: **Waiter, this food isn't fit for a pig.**
Waiter: Sorry, sir. I'll bring you some that is.

What's green and pecks on trees?
Woody Woodpickle.

What's the hamburger's theme song?
"Home on the Range."

What did one hamburger say to the other hamburger?
"Hey, nice buns!"

What day of the week do hamburgers hate?
Fry day.

Harry: Aren't you going to eat lunch today?
Carrie: No, I'm putting on too much weight.
Harry: How can you tell?
Carrie: My mom had to let out the shower curtain.

Two Martians land on Earth. They are walking down the street eating garbage cans, and one says to the other, "The crusts are good, but the fillings are awfully rich."

Who grows cucumbers for the pickle factory?
The farmer in the dill.

Why is a vegetable garden the worst place to keep secrets?
Because the potatoes have eyes and the beanstalk.

What kind of fish goes best with a peanut-butter sandwich?
Jellyfish.

What's white on the outside, green on the inside, and jumps?
A frog sandwich.

What's brown on the outside, green on the inside, and jumps?
A frog sandwich on toast.

What's black and white and green every afternoon?
A zebra that eats in the school cafeteria.

**ONLY 43
MORE PAGES
TILL YOU GET TO
THE WORLD'S
DIRTIEST JOKE!**

KNOCK-OUT
KNOCK KNOCKS

Knock knock.
Who's there?
A.
A who?
A you, hurry up and open the door!

Knock knock.
Who's there?
B.
B who?
B a nice guy and open the door, willya?

Knock knock.
Who's there?
C.
C who?
C me standing out here? Open the door!

Knock knock.
Who's there?
D.
D who?
D-lighted to make your acquaintance, if you'll only open the door!

Knock knock.
Who's there?
E.
E who?
E-zy does it when you open that door!

Knock knock.
Who's there?
F.
F who?
F you don't open the door, I'll kick it down.

Knock knock.
Who's there?
G.
G who?
G whiz, I've been standing out here a long time.

Knock knock.
Who's there?
H.
H who?
H-ya ever gonna open this door?

Knock knock.
Who's there?
I.
I who?
I quit.

BE A SPORT!

Q: What's furry, hibernates, and can slam dunk a basketball?

A: "Bear" Jordan.

The baseball team had spent the whole season in last place, and the manager was desperate. One day, a horse came to his office. "I want to play on your team," the horse said.

The manager was very surprised. But finally he said, "Why not? What have I got to lose?"

The next game, the horse was the starting pitcher. In the first inning, he struck out the other side. He struck out every batter in the second and third innings too.

In the bottom of the third, the horse came up to bat. He hit the first pitch deep into centerfield. It bounced near the wall. The centerfielder had trouble getting it, but finally he threw it to the infield.

The shortstop dropped it, picked it up, and threw to first. The throw was wild. The second baseman chased after it, finally grabbed it, then threw to first. The ball got to first before the horse did, and he was out.

The horse went back to the dugout. "You know," the manager told him, "you're a terrific pitcher. And you can really slug the ball. But you're the slowest runner I've ever seen!"

And the horse replied, "If I could run, do you think I'd be here?"

Q: Who can go as fast as a racehorse?
A: The jockey!

Will: Look—I just found a lost football.
Bill: How do you know it's lost?
Will: Because the kids down the street are still looking for it!

Q: What is served hundreds of times but never eaten?
A: A tennis ball.

Q: What has long floppy ears and can slam dunk a basketball?
A: "Hare" Jordan.

Q: What disease can you catch from a martial arts expert?

A: Kung Flu.

Q: What has 18 legs and catches flies?
A: A baseball team.

Matt: Are you going to the baseball game with me this afternoon?
June: No. It's a waste of time. I can tell you the score before the game starts.
Matt: Oh, yeah? What is it then?
June: Nothing to nothing!

Q: Why was Cinderella such a lousy basketball player?
A: She had a pumpkin for a coach!

Q: Why are the players always hot at the end of a baseball game?
A: Because all the fans leave.

Q: Who has long black hair, tattoos, and can slam dunk a basketball?
A: "Cher Jordan."

THESE JOKES ARE SICK

Wife: Doctor, my husband thinks he's a dog.

Doctor: How long has this been going on?

Wife: Ever since he was a puppy!

A man goes to a doctor with a pain in his arm. The doctor spends ten minutes examining the arm. Then he says, "Tell me, sir, have you ever had this pain before?"

"Yes, I have," the man answers.

"Well, you've got it again!"

Doctor: Here, house. Here, house.
Nurse: **What are you doing?**
Doctor: Making a house call!

A woman goes to a psychiatrist. "Doctor," she says, "you've got to help me. Nobody ever pays any attention to me. Sometimes I feel as though I'm invisible."

And the doctor says, "Next!"

Wife: Doctor, my husband eats grapes all day long.
Doctor: **What's wrong with that?**
Wife: Off the wallpaper?

Mother: Doctor, my son thinks he's a chicken.

Doctor: That's terrible. Why didn't you bring him to see me?"

Mother: I would have, but we need the eggs."

A man had stomach pains so he went to see his doctor for an X-ray. "Good heavens, man!" the doctor cried. "There's a wristwatch in your stomach!"

"Yeah, I know, Doc. I swallowed it when I was twelve."

"Hasn't it given you any trouble before?" the doctor asked.

"Only when I wind it."

Patient: I have a terrible problem, Doctor. I keep losing my memory.

Doctor: How long have you had this problem?

Patient: What problem?

"Doctor, my husband thinks he's a washing machine. He rolls his head around and around, and hot water and soap come out his ears."

"I don't think he's really doing any harm."

"You don't understand, Doctor—he isn't getting the sheets clean!"

ANIMAL HOWLS

Q: What's the best way to catch a fish?

A: Have someone throw it to you.

Q: **What do you call a chocolate-covered sheep?**

A: A candy baa.

Q: **How do you keep a skunk from smelling?**

A: Hold its nose.

Q: **What did the bird say when its cage broke?**

A: "Cheap cheap cheap!"

Q: **What happens when one electric eel kisses another?**

A: It's a shocking experience.

Q: **What do you get when you cross a turkey with a centipede?**

A: The perfect Thanksgiving meal—drumsticks for everyone.

April: There's a ten-foot snake in the cage over there.

June: You can't fool me. Snakes don't have feet!

April: Did you know that an elephant never forgets?

May: Big deal! What has an elephant got to remember?

Q: What does a 500-pound mouse say?

A: "Here, kitty, kitty . . ."

Q: What does a duck wear to the prom?

A: A duxedo.

Q: What do you call a mouse that steps on a lion's paw?

A: Dinner.

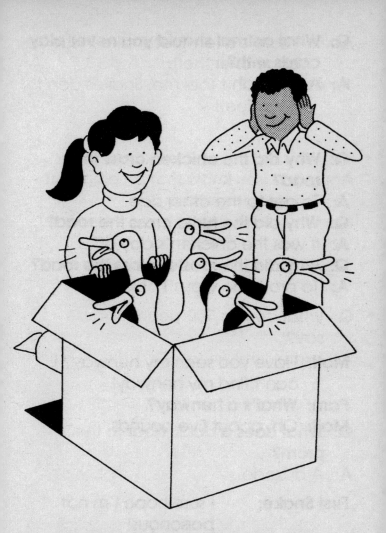

Q: What do you get when you put ducks in a cardboard container?

A: A box of quackers.

Q: What animal should you never play cards with?

A: A cheetah.

Q: Why did the chicken cross the road?

A: To get to the other side.

Q: Why did the turtle cross the road?

A: It was the chicken's day off.

Q: Why did the rooster cross the road?

A: To prove he wasn't chicken!

Matt: Have you seen my henway? I can't find my henway!

Pam: What's a henway?

Matt: Oh, about five pounds.

First Snake: I sure hope I'm not poisonous!

Second Snake: How come?

First Snake: Because I just bit my tongue.

Pam: Hey, don't give my cat lemon.
Sam: **Why not?**
Pam: I don't want her to become a
sourpuss!

Sam: **Boy, that last joke was awful.**
Pam: Yeah, it was a real lemon!

Q: **Where do polar bears keep their money?**
A: In a snow bank.

Q: **What did the beaver say after he cut down the tree?**
A: "Nice gnawing you."

Q: **What is a bee's favorite candy?**
A: Bumblegum.

Q: **What do turtles wear in winter?**
A: People-neck sweaters.

Q: How do you send a whale cross-country?

A: In a whale-road car.

Q: What did the leopard say after a great dinner?

A: "That really hit the spots!"

Two mice were chatting in a laboratory. "And how are you getting along with the professor?" said one.

"Oh, excellently. I've got him thoroughly trained. Every time I ring the bell, he brings me food."

Q: What did the judge say when a skunk walked into the room?

A: "Odor in the court!"

Q: What do you get when you cross a duck with a rooster?

A: An animal that wakes you up at the quack of dawn!

Q: What's the difference between an elephant and a grape?

A: One is gray, the other is purple.

Q: What did Tarzan say when he saw the elephants coming?

A: "The grapes are coming! The grapes are coming!" (He was color blind.)

DO-IT-YOURSELF JOKES

Customize these jokes to suit yourself. What goes in the blank depends on your mood. Try "the principal." Try "the third grader." Try "my little sister." It's your choice.

Example: Why did <u>my little</u> <u>sister</u> **stand in front** of the mirror with her eyes closed?

She wanted to see how she looked when she was asleep.

Another example: Why was <u>the</u> <u>principal</u> **so late for school?**

He was stuck for three hours on an escalator.

Now try these:

Why did _____

_____

bring Band-Aids to the picnic?
For the cold cuts.

Why did _____

_____ **drive**

his car through the restaurant doors?
He was on a crash diet.

Why was _____

_____ **late for school?**

He was dreaming about basketball,
and the game went into overtime.

What are the three most difficult years

in school for _____

_____?

Second grade.

Why did _____

_____buy

birdseed when he didn't have a bird?

He wanted to plant it and grow one.

TWO TOO CRUEL

Mother: Chris, why is your little brother crying?

Chris: Because I won't give him any of my candy.

Mother: But I gave both of you candy. Is his gone already?

Chris: Yes, and he cried the whole time I was eating it.

"Has your grand piano arrived yet?"

"Yes, isn't it grand? It came yesterday. We hitched it to the cat, and she pulled it up to the third floor."

"How could a little cat like that drag a grand piano up two floors?"

"We used a whip!"

MORE KNOCK-OUT KNOCK KNOCKS

Knock knock.
Who's there?
Koala.
Koala who?
Koala the cops—I've been robbed!

Knock knock.
Who's there?
Yvonne.
Yvonne who?
Yvonne to suck your blood!

Knock knock.
Who's there?
Alaska.
Alaska who?
Alaska who she is next time!

Knock knock.
Who's there?
Ben.
Ben who?
Benana split sounds good for dessert!

Knock knock.
Who's there?
Boo.
Boo who?
Why are you crying?

Knock knock.
Who's there?
You.
You who?
Yoo hoo to you too!

Knock knock.
Who's there?
Hitch.
Hitch who?
Gesundheit!

Knock knock.
Who's there?
Lettuce.
Lettuce who?
Lettuce in, willya! We're tired of knocking!

Knock knock.
Who's there?
Isabelle.
Isabelle who?
Isabelle ringing?

Knock knock.
Who's there?
Wendy.
Wendy who?
Wendy you think you'll open the door?

Knock knock.
Who's there?
Noah.
Noah who?
Noah place I can find some better
knock-knock jokes?

SCHOOL JOKES WITH CLASS

Teacher: How would you find the English Channel?

Chuck: I can't. We don't have cable.

Teacher: If you have fifty apples in one hand and forty apples in the other hand, what do you have?

Chuck: Big hands!

Teacher: If you take two from five, what's the difference?

Sam: I agree. What's the difference?

Teacher: Why is it so difficult for you to learn how to spell?

Will: Because you keep changing the words!

Teacher: Marvin, this story you turned in called "Our Cat" is exactly the same as your brother's story.

Marvin: What do you expect? It's the same cat!

Will: Yaaay! The teacher said we'd have a test today rain or shine!

Bill: Then why are you so happy?

Will: It's snowing!

Q: What's the hardest part of a test?

A: The answers.

Pam: Why are you so upset?

Sam: The teacher yelled at me for something I didn't do.

Pam: How unfair. What was it?

Sam: My homework.

Teacher: Will you two stop passing notes?

Matt: We're not passing notes, we're playing cards.

Teacher: Marvin, I hope I didn't see you looking at Amy's paper.

Marvin: I hope you didn't either!

Will: I've decided to go to night school.

Bill: Why?

Will: I want to learn how to read in the dark.

69

Teacher: Can anyone tell me when the Mississippi River was found?

Marvin: I didn't even know it was lost!

Fred: I'm not going to school today, Mom. Nobody there likes me.

Mother: Don't be silly, Fred. Besides, you have to go. You're the principal!

Teacher: What did George Washington say to his soldiers before crossing the Delaware River?

Marvin: "Get into the boat!"

Teacher: Can anyone tell me what George Washington, Abraham Lincoln, and Christopher Columbus have in common?

Matt: They were all born on holidays.

Marvin: Teacher, I ain't got a pencil.

Teacher: I *haven't* got a pencil.

Marvin: That makes two of us!

Teacher: Marvin, this is the fifth day this week I've had to punish you. What do you have to say for yourself?

Marvin: Thank goodness it's Friday!

Q: What did one math book say to another?

A: "Boy, have I got problems!"

ONLY 6
MORE PAGES
TILL YOU GET TO
THE WORLD'S
DIRTIEST JOKE!

RIDDLE-DICULOUS RIDDLES

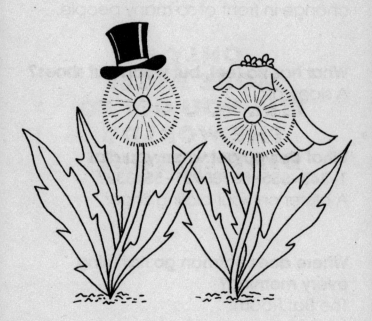

What do you call two dandelions that just got married?
Newlyweeds.

Where does Friday come before Thursday?
In a dictionary.

Why did the traffic light turn red?
It was embarrassed at having to change in front of so many people.

What has no feet, but wears out shoes?
A sidewalk.

What do you get when you dial 1-345-555-56780921-554332?
A blister on your dialing finger.

Where does Batman go first thing every morning?
The Bat Room.

What did the digital watch say to its mother?
"Look Ma, no hands!"

How do you know if a Tyrannosaurus Rex is asleep?
You can hear its dinosnores.

Why was the belt in jail?
It held up a pair of pants.

What kind of truck gets stepped on the most?
A tow truck!

Why did King Kong climb up the Empire State Building?
He couldn't fit into the elevator.

What is NBC?
A dumb way to start the alphabet.

Harry: Why is 6 scared of 7?
Carrie: Because 7 8 9.

What goes "zzub, zzub, zzub"?
A bee flying backward.

What did the Martian say to the gas pump?

"Take your finger out of your ear and listen to me."

HERE IT IS, THE WORLD'S DIRTIEST JOKE...

A WHITE HORSE